More than Words

More than Words

ROBERT MORRIS

STUDY GUIDE

GATEWAY®
PRESS

More than Words Study Guide
Copyright © 2019 by Robert Morris

ISBN: 978-1-949399-65-3

We hope you hear from the Holy Spirit and receive God's richest blessings
from this book by Gateway Press. We want to provide the highest quality
resources that take the messages, music, and media of Gateway Church
to the world. For more information on other resources from Gateway
Publishing®, go to gatewaypublishing.com.

Gateway Press, an imprint of Gateway Publishing
700 Blessed Way
Southlake, Texas 76092
gatewaypublishing.com

19 20 21 22 23   5 4 3 2 1

CONTENTS

1

BREAD

The Bible is the bread of life. It is our daily bread, our sustaining bread, and the true bread.

ENGAGE

If you had the option, would you rather spend one day in the past or one day in the future?

WATCH

Watch "Bread."

- Look for the different functions of the bread of life.
- Consider how the bread sustains us and why we should read the Bible on a daily basis.

(If you are not able to watch this teaching on video, read the following. Otherwise, skip to the **Talk** section after viewing.)

READ

This is a series about the Bible. The purpose of the series is to help us better understand God's Word. And the Bible *is* God's Word. I once heard a professed Christian say that we should interpret the Bible the way we interpret other major works of literature, like Shakespeare. I was shocked. That is not the doctrine of biblical interpretation. The doctrine of biblical interpretation is the opposite: the Bible is of *no* personal interpretation. Let me put it this way: You don't interpret the Bible. The Bible interprets you.

> Once you decide the Bible is inspired by God, you know it is inerrant and infallible. I will show you how you know that for sure.

There is a whole move now against the inerrancy of Scripture, but it is the same argument that was used 30 or 60 years ago: that there are inconsistencies. Yes, I believe that it is scientifically impossible for a man to live inside the body of a fish for three days, for a sea to part on its own into dry land, or for a man to walk on water. It's scientifically impossible for a man to be raised from the dead. That doesn't prove that the Bible is not true. It proves that God is God. God is not a God of science. The first attack of Satan was to question the word of God. That leads to you becoming God. If you can decide which passages are inspired and which passages are not, that means you become God. And you're not God.

This is the next attack of the enemy because he doesn't have to attack issues anymore if he can attack and cast doubt on God's Word.

This message is about how God's Word is spiritual bread for us.

Our Daily Bread

The Bible is our daily bread.

Then the Lord said to Moses, "Behold, I will rain bread from heaven for you. And the people shall go out and gather a certain quota every day, that I may test them, whether they will walk in My law or not" (Exodus 16:4).

Note the words "bread from heaven." When God sent manna for the children of Israel, He provided it daily. This is important because Jesus also teaches this. Matthew 6:11 says, "Give us this day our daily bread." Yes, this is talking about provision, but since the Bible is bread, it also refers to a daily word from God.

When we don't eat, we feel tired and weak. I think some Christians feel tired and weak because they don't eat every day. Psalm 68:19 says, "Blessed be the Lord, who daily loads us with benefits." I'd like us to make a commitment to read the Bible every day. It's easy to do, and it's free.

There are three types of Bibles. One is a paraphrase, like The Living Bible. It takes the English version and puts it into modern day language. Translations go back to the original Hebrew Old

Testament and Greek New Testament. There are two types of translations. An "exact equivalency" translates word by word. A "dynamic equivalency" translates the phrase or thought. I preach from the New King James Version because it is exact equivalency, and I like to know what the exact word means in the Greek or Hebrew. You can read whichever version you prefer.

Our Sustaining Bread

Now when the tempter came to Him, he said, "If You are the Son of God, command that these stones become bread." But He answered and said, "It is written, 'Man shall not live by bread alone, but by every word that proceeds from the mouth of God'" (Matthew 4:3-4).

A word from His Word every day sustains us. Jesus used Scripture to overcome the devil. Three times when Jesus was tempted, He said, "It is written." This passage shows that the Bible is our spiritual bread. He was quoting Deuteronomy 8:3:

> "So He humbled you, allowed you to hunger, and fed you with manna which you did not know nor did your fathers know, that He might make you know that man shall not live by bread alone; but man lives by every *word* that proceeds from the mouth of the Lord."

We need physical food to sustain our physical bodies. We need spiritual food to sustain our spiritual bodies. A whole bunch of

Christians are dying from spiritual malnutrition. Isaiah 55:2 says that when we eat spiritual bread, our soul will "delight itself in abundance." Job 23:12 and Joshua 1:8 express similar ideas. Joshua says that if you meditate on the Word day and night, "you will make your way prosperous ... and then you will have good success." If the Bible will make you prosper, then reading it is the most important thing that you can do every day.

Our True Bread

In John 6, Jesus reminded the crowd that God gave manna in the desert to their forefathers after they left Egypt. It is bread from heaven.

> Then Jesus said to them, "Most assuredly, I say to you, Moses did not give you the bread from heaven, but My Father gives you the true bread from heaven. For the bread of God is He who comes down from heaven and gives life to the world."
>
> Then they said to Him, "Lord, give us this bread always."
>
> And Jesus said to them, "I am the bread of life. He who comes to Me shall never hunger, and he who believes in Me shall never thirst. ... I am the bread of life. Your fathers ate the manna in the wilderness, and are dead. This is the bread which comes down from heaven, that one may eat of it and not die. I am the living bread which came down from heaven. If anyone eats of this bread, he will live forever; and the bread that I shall give is My flesh, which I shall give for the life of the world" (John 6:32-35, 48-51).

The manna was bread of life, but Jesus is **the** *bread of life.*
John 1:1 says, "In the beginning was the Word, and the Word
was with God, and the Word was God." John 1:14 says the
"Word became flesh." Revelation 19:13 says, "His name is called
the Word of God."

When you read the Bible, you are taking in Jesus. Jesus said in
John 6:63, "The words I speak to you are spirit, and they are life."
The more you read the Bible, the more Jesus gets in you. We have
the key to everything. The secrets to miracles. God's autobiography
and the encyclopedia of life. We have the answer to every problem.
And it's an app on our phone that we seldom open. When we read
God's Word, we are receiving the life and power of Jesus.

NOTES

_____

_____

_____

_____

_____

_____

TALK

These questions can be used for group discussion or personal reflection.

Question 1
Read John 6:32–35, 48–51. How is Jesus like bread?

_____

_____

_____

_____

Question 2
In the Old Testament, God sent manna on a daily basis. Why is it important to have a daily routine of reading the Bible? How does it affect us when we do *and* when we don't have our "daily bread"?

_____

_____

_____

_____

Question 3
Read Matthew 4:3–4. When Jesus was tempted, He used the Bible to overcome the enemy. Share about a time you were going

through a difficulty and how some key Scriptures helped get you through it. How did that affect you?

_____

_____

_____

_____

Question 4
Have you ever read the Bible and known God was speaking directly to you about a situation in your life?

Be Still & Know that I Am God.

_____

_____

PRAY

If studying alone, ask the Holy Spirit to reveal the truth about Himself to you. If in a group, take some time to pray for each other as you think about the truths discussed in this session.

EXPLORE

Do you want to go deeper with this teaching? Here are some additional things to think about, pray for, or write about in your journal throughout the next week.

Key Quote

> *You don't interpret the Bible. The Bible interprets you.*

What are some current areas of your life in which you need help? Take time this week to find some specific Scriptures that speak to your situation.

_____

_____

_____

_____

_____

Key Verses

Exodus 16:14; John 6:31-51; Matthew 4:3-4

What truths stand out to you as you read these verses?

_____

_____

_____

What is the Holy Spirit saying to you through these Scriptures?

_____

_____

_____

Key Question
What are some practical ways to memorize Scripture and apply it to your life?

Key Prayer
Heavenly Father, thank You for sending Jesus, the True Bread of Life. Thank You for giving us the written Word so we can partake of the bread of life. Help us to take in daily the Scriptures, our sustaining bread. In Jesus' name, Amen.

2

WATER

Water is vital to sustaining life. The Bible—the Word of God—is a nourishing and cleansing water.

RECAP

In the previous session, we saw the importance of the Bible as the believer's daily bread that God provides to sustain and nourish us.

Did you read the Bible more this week? How did the Word of God sustain you through the week?

ENGAGE

Do you enjoy gardening? Do you have a green thumb or a brown one?

WATCH

Watch "Water."

- Look for the ways Satan tries to attack us.
- Consider the function of water in the life of a Christian.

(If you are not able to watch this teaching on video, read the following. Otherwise, skip to the **Talk** section after viewing.)

READ

In the last session, we saw how the Bible is bread to us. The Bible is also our water. Both of them nourish us. According to experts, we can go without food for perhaps 40 to 80 days. We can go without water for perhaps 4 to 14 days. It depends on physical condition. If the Bible is food and water, how long can you go spiritually without this book? I know our spirits are saved and sealed by the Holy Spirit, but I think we have a lot of malnourished Christians. They're not eating their bread and drinking their water daily.

God ties bread and water together to mean the Word of God.

The people asked, and He brought quail,
And satisfied them with the bread of heaven.
He opened the rock, and water gushed out;
It ran in the dry places *like* a river (Psalm 105:40-41).

There was literal bread, represented by manna. The literal rock also represented something spiritual. The rock "followed them." That would probably scare you as much as a burning bush. The Bible is a spiritual book, written by spiritual beings, to spiritual beings. That's why science has such a hard time understanding it. The Bible is *full* of spiritual meanings, which is why it is so important for you to read it. It's not a history book. It's not a literature book—it's an autobiography from God!

The rock and water have spiritual meanings.

> And all drank the same spiritual drink. For they drank of that spiritual Rock that followed them, and that Rock was Christ (1 Corinthians 10:4).

They drank literal water, and that water was spiritual drink. And they drank of that spiritual rock that followed them—that rock was Christ. And, by the way, the cloud that went before them by day, and the fire by night, was the Holy Spirit.

There is a war of words going on in our lives every day. The question is, *Whose word are you going to believe?* God is telling you what happened and what's true. Satan is saying, "Did God really say that?" Here is the war of words. Satan wants to flood us and famish us. God wants to fill us.

Satan Tries to Flood Us

> So the great dragon was cast out, that serpent of old, called the
> Devil and Satan, who deceives the whole world; he was cast to the
> earth, and his angels were cast out with him (Revelation 12:9).

There is no question here that the serpent is Satan, the devil.
Now look at verse 15:

> So the serpent spewed water out of his mouth like a flood after the
> woman, that he might cause her to be carried away by the flood.

The woman is the type of the Church.

What comes out of your mouth? Words. Satan spews water—
words—out of his mouth to cause you to be carried away. I'm
sure you've had a flood of words come against you at some time:
"You're not going to live long." "You married the wrong person."
"God doesn't like you." How about, "You're crazy"? Satan's
accusing words relentlessly attack our health, relationships,
finances, and many other areas of our lives.

Water represents words. In Psalm 69:1–2 David writes,

> Save me, O God!
> For the waters have come up to *my* neck.
> I sink in deep mire,

Where *there is* no standing;
I have come into deep waters,
Where the floods overflow me."

David says over and over that his enemies are coming against him.
A flood of words is coming against him. "You're not going to be king."
"Absalom is going to take the throne from you." "God's punishing you
for your sin." That's one we all hear. God cannot punish you for your
sin if you've accepted Jesus, because He's already punished Jesus.

Psalm 93:3 says, "The floods have lifted up their voice." The
floods represent the words of the enemy. But in verse 4 God says,
"The Lord on high *is* mightier / Than the noise of many waters, /
Than the mighty waves of the sea." In Matthew 7 Jesus likens the
Word to a wise man who built his house on a *rock*, and when the
floods came, it did not fall. It was founded on the *rock*—Jesus.

Satan can talk, God can talk, and we can talk. Our mouths also
get us in trouble. Our words are water, and we can drown ourselves.
Proverbs 18:4 says, "The words of a man's mouth are deep waters."
You can talk yourself into falling. And Proverbs 18:21 says that "death
and life are in the power of the tongue." This means that God speaks
words of life, Satan speaks words of death, and I have the power to
agree with one of them. I can agree with the One who speaks life
over me, or I can agree with the one who speaks death over me.
So now death and life are in the power of my tongue. Isaiah 59:19
declares that the Spirit of the Lord will lift up a standard against
the enemy when he comes in like a flood. The Bible is our standard.

Three times Jesus quoted Scripture to overcome temptation. If Jesus uses the Bible to overcome temptation, how much more do you need to use the Bible to overcome temptation? Just quote the Bible.

Satan Tries to Famish Us

Amos 8:11 says,

> "Behold, the days are coming," says the Lord God,
> "That I will send a famine on the land,
> Not a famine of bread,
> Nor a thirst for water,
> But of hearing the words of the Lord."

This is a spiritual famine, not a natural famine. And it is a famine of not *hearing* the words of the Lord—not a famine of the words themselves. There are plenty of words of God. The problem is us not hearing them. Joshua 1:8 and Psalm 1 say that for those who lean on the Lord, who meditate on His Word, whatever he does prospers. This does not mean financial prosperity, but the carrying and removal of your burdens. Health, finances, children, career—whatever the burden may be. If we believed that, we'd meditate on it a lot more.

Mark 4:14-15 says that Satan comes immediately to take away the word that is sown in our hearts. How can Satan take the word out of my heart? The mouth speaks "from the abundance of the heart." So God sows the word in our hearts. When He does, Satan immediately tries to get us to say something in opposition to God's word. When we do, His word leaves our heart. Because I'm the one that spoke it out. Satan starves us by preventing us from reading and understanding the Bible.

Jesus Wants to Fill Us

> These things we also speak, not in words which man's wisdom teaches but which the Holy Spirit teaches, comparing spiritual things with spiritual. But the natural man does not receive the things of the Spirit of God, for they are foolishness to him; nor can he know *them,* because they are spiritually discerned (1 Corinthians 2:13-14).

There are two conversations: natural and spiritual. Whoever reads the Bible with natural eyes will never understand it. Here is an example of the natural and spiritual conversation from John 4:

> A woman of Samaria came to draw water. Jesus said to her, "Give Me a drink." For His disciples had gone away into the city to buy food.
> Then the woman of Samaria said to Him, "How is it that You, being a Jew, ask a drink from me, a Samaritan woman?" For Jews have no dealings with Samaritans.
> Jesus answered and said to her, "If you knew the gift of God, and who it is who says to you, 'Give Me a drink,' you would have asked Him, and He would have given you living water" (vv. 7-10).

You see the spiritual conversation from Jesus. Then she goes right back to the natural conversation:

> The woman said to Him, "Sir, You have nothing to draw with, and the well is deep. Where then do You get that living water? Are You greater than our father Jacob, who gave us the well, and drank from it himself, as well as his sons and his livestock?" (vv. 11-12).

Logic says this ... science says this. Then Jesus says,

> "Whoever drinks of this water will thirst again, but whoever drinks of the water that I shall give him will never thirst. But the water that I shall give him will become in him a fountain of water springing up into everlasting life" (vv. 13-14).

Whoever drinks of this natural water will thirst again. But, Jesus says, the water I will give brings everlasting life.

If they're looking at the situation with natural eyes, this is what the conversation will look like. But Jesus says, "I'm not talking about natural water. I'm talking about spiritual water." It will become a fountain *inside* of you. The fountain washes us from the inside. Ephesians 5:26 says we are cleansed "with the washing of water by the word." The water is in your mind, will, and emotions. If you read the Bible every day, it will cleanse your soul. Take a bath in the word. Every day. Just read at least one chapter a day and meditate on one passage a day.

NOTES

_____

_____

_____

_____

_____

TALK

These questions can be used for group discussion or personal reflection.

Question 1
Read 1 Corinthians 10:4. What kind of drink does Paul mention and from what kind of rock? Who is the Rock? When we spend time reading the Word of God, how are we nourishing ourselves?

_____

_____

_____

_____

Question 2
In Psalm 93:3-4, we read that floods lift up their voice, but who is mightier? What hope do you find from this verse?

_____

_____

_____

_____

Question 3

Read Joshua 1:8 and Psalm 1:2-3. What are those who meditate on the Word of God promised?

_____

_____

_____

_____

Question 4

In John 4:7-14, what type of water does Jesus reference? Why does the Samaritan woman not understand?

_____

_____

_____

_____

Question 5

How are we cleansed? Read Ephesians 5:25-26. When we allow this to happen, how does this affect our thoughts?

_____

_____

_____

_____

PRAY

If studying alone, ask the Holy Spirit to reveal the truth about Himself to you. If in a group, take some time to pray for each other as you think about the truths discussed in this session.

EXPLORE

Do you want to go deeper with this teaching? Here are some additional things to think about, pray for, or write about in your journal throughout the next week.

Key Quote

> *God speaks words of life, Satan speaks words of death, and I have the power to agree with one of them.*

What words have you spoke recently that were identifiable as life or death words?

_____

_____

_____

_____

_____

Key Verses
Revelation 12; Psalm 69; Psalm 93:3-4; John 4:7-14;
Ephesians 5:25-26.

What truths stand out to you as you read these verses?

_____

_____

_____

What is the Holy Spirit saying to you through these Scriptures?

_____

_____

_____

Key Question
Sometimes, we overwhelm ourselves with words. How did Jesus
deal with a flood of words from Satan?

Key Prayer
Lord, thank You for making a way for me to receive the gift of
salvation and for me to be victorious against the attack of the
enemy. Help me to recognize the enemy's flooding words and to
defend myself with Your Word. Lord, thank You for the gift of
Your Word that cleanses me, fills me, and quenches my spiritual
thirst. In Jesus' name, Amen.

3

BREATH

Just like we cannot live by only breathing on the weekends, neither can we spiritually thrive by receiving the Word only on the weekends. We must breathe deeply and inhale the Word of God every day.

RECAP

In the previous session, we saw that we are nourished by spiritual water. Satan's words accuse us, and our own words can also harm us. Jesus, however, wants to fill us with living, spiritual water.

How did you speak this week? Were you more aware of the nature of your words and the words of others?

ENGAGE

Do you have a memorable Easter egg hunt?

WATCH

Watch "Breath."

- Look for how God brings things into being.
- Consider the different things that God's breath brings to us.

(If you are not able to watch this teaching on video, read the following. Otherwise, skip to the **Talk** section after viewing.)

READ

The first part of this message deals with some theological things that need to be said today. The Bible is more than words. It is the Word of God. There is an attack against the Bible going on today. This next wave of attack of the enemy is to disqualify the Bible.

The Bible is the very breath of God. We've talked about the Bible being our life-sustaining nourishment (bread) and the water of life. Breath is like air. We can live without food for 40 to 80 days and without water for 3 to 14 days. You can only go without air for a few minutes at most. I think we have many malnourished, dehydrated, and oxygen-depleted Christians. They're not eating their bread, they're not drinking their water, and they're not breathing in the breath of God.

Why do we call it the breath of God? Look at 2 Timothy 3:16:

All Scripture *is* given by inspiration of God, and *is* profitable for
doctrine, for reproof, for correction, for instruction in righteousness.

The five words "given by inspiration of God" are one word in the
Greek: *theopneustos*. It is made up of two Greek words. *Theo* means
'God.' *Pneuma* means 'breath,' and then *pneustos* means 'breathe.'
One version (NIV) translates it literally as "God-breathed."
Scripture is *breathed* by God. That's what we call the inspiration of
Scripture. *Inspire* means literally to *breathe in*. The primary meaning
of *expire* is to breathe out. (Both English words have secondary
meanings, of course.) God not only inspired the Scripture (breathed
it into the men who wrote it), but He also expired it, because He
breathed it out in order to breathe it into them.

Second Peter 1:20-21 says, "Knowing this first, that no prophecy
of Scripture is of any private interpretation, for prophecy never
came by the will of man, but holy men of God spoke *as they were
moved* by the Holy Spirit." The Holy Spirit—God—breathed out
the Word of God, He breathed it into men, and they wrote as they
were inspired—or filled—with the breath of God. This is important:
If Scripture came from the mouth of God, it can't have errors in it.
If you deny the inerrancy of Scripture, you will also have to deny
the inspiration of Scripture. God can't make mistakes. And if it has
errors, then you can pick and choose which parts are right. That
makes you God. And you're not. And one day, the Bible will judge
you. And Jesus said that if anyone speaks against the Holy Spirit, it
will never be forgiven Him, in this lifetime or the age to come.

Some people feel that there must be errors because some versions of the Bible contain contradictions. This is a big issue. To understand contradictions, you must understand the laws of logic. The second law of logic is the law of non-contradiction (LNC). This law says that there can be two expressions of the same event, and as long as one does not exclude the possibility of the other, then it is not a contradiction. In other words, you can have two different statements about an event from two different people, and as long as one statement does not prove the other to be false, then there is no contradiction.

There are two Scriptures that are commonly used to claim a contradiction in the Bible.

First, Matthew says that Judas went out and hung himself. He gets right to the bottom line. Luke, writing in Acts 1, says that Judas flung himself headlong into a field, and his entrails burst open (spilled out).

Those don't contradict. Judas did hang himself—the day before the Sabbath. Judas's body remained there for some time, during which his body would have started to decompose, and gases began to build up in his stomach. His body would have begun to get bloated. No otherwise healthy person ever just fell headfirst and their stomach burst open.

Not long ago, after a dead whale was recovered from a beach and was on its way to the laboratory, the whale's stomach burst open, and the people watching along the road were covered with the whale's intestines.

So the explanation was simple: Judas hung himself, and the body began to decompose while hanging in the sun. They cut him down on the next day. He fell headlong (because a man's center of gravity is above the waist). So Matthew, the tax collector, says Judas went out and hung himself. Luke, the *physician*, says this man fell headlong and his entrails fell out. These are just two different perspectives of the same story.

I can't make you believe in God, or that the Bible is the Word of God. You have to have faith. But once you do believe, your life is changed forever, because you have a standard now. You also have life.

Ezekiel 37:1–10 is the Scripture reference for our four points about the breath of God:

> The hand of the Lord came upon me and brought me out in the Spirit of the Lord, and set me down in the midst of the valley; and it *was* full of bones. Then He caused me to pass by them all around, and behold, *there were* very many in the open valley; and indeed *they were* very dry. And He said to me, "Son of man, can these bones live?"
>
> So I answered, "O Lord God, You know."
>
> Again He said to me, "Prophesy to these bones, and say to them, 'O dry bones, hear the word of the Lord! Thus says the Lord God to these bones: "Surely I will cause breath to enter into you, and you shall live. I will put sinews on you and bring flesh upon you, cover you with skin and put breath in you; and you shall live. Then you shall know that I *am* the Lord."'"

So I prophesied as I was commanded; and as I prophesied, there was a noise, and suddenly a rattling; and the bones came together, bone to bone. Indeed, as I looked, the sinews and the flesh came upon them, and the skin covered them over; but *there was* no breath in them.

Also He said to me, "Prophesy to the breath, prophesy, son of man, and say to the breath, 'Thus says the Lord God: "Come from the four winds, O breath, and breathe on these slain, that they may live."'" So I prophesied as He commanded me, and breath came into them, and they lived, and stood upon their feet, an exceedingly great army.

Note that these were bones, not skeletons. They were unattached.

The Breath of God Brings Understanding

Verse 3 says, "O Lord God, You know." You can't judge the Bible by whether you'll understand it or not. There are things you won't understand, but you have to believe by faith. Job 32:8 says, "But *there is* a spirit in man, / And the breath of the Almighty gives him understanding." We've all said at some time, "If I could just understand what God is trying to teach me right now." The Bible is what gives you understanding. When we read the Bible, God gives us understanding. Read the owner's manual from the Manufacturer.

The Breath of God Brings Order

Scripture brings order. Verse 7 says "the bones came together, bone to bone." The skeletons were formed from the breath of God—by the Word of God. Psalm 33:6 says that the heavens were made by the word and the breath from God's mouth. Genesis 1:2-3 says He spoke light into existence. It brought order to the chaos. Things came into order when God spoke.

The Breath of God Brings Strength

In verses 6 and 8, God put the sinews (tendons that connect the bone to muscle) and flesh upon the skeletons. God brought structure and order to life and gave it power. You need something to connect you to the power of God. The Word of God connects you. When you worship in Spirit and truth—when you combine reading the Bible with receiving the Holy Spirit—you're going to walk in the power of God.

In Exodus 15:8-10, after crossing the Red Sea, the Israelites sang this song:

And with the blast of Your nostrils
The waters were gathered together;
The floods stood upright like a heap;
The depths congealed in the heart of the sea.
The enemy said, 'I will pursue,
I will overtake,
I will divide the spoil;

My desire shall be satisfied on them.
I will draw my sword,
My hand shall destroy them.'
You blew with Your wind,
The sea covered them;
They sank like lead in the mighty waters.

God blew with His wind. That is how God parted the Red Sea with a breath from His nostrils, and He covered it over again the same way.

The Breath of God Brings Life

"So I prophesied as He commanded me, and breath came into them, and they lived" (Ezekiel 37:10).

When you read the Bible, you get understanding. Your life comes into order. You get the power of God in your life. And you get life itself. You're filled with the breath of God. Job 33:4 says, "The Spirit of God has made me, / And the breath of the Almighty gives me life." In Genesis 2:7 it says God "breathed into his [Adam's] nostrils the breath of life."

When I prepare my lessons each week, I breathe into myself the Word of God, and when I come to preach each week, I breathe out what God has breathed into me. And you receive the life of God. But one breath a week is not enough for you.

This week, for God's sake, eat some bread, take a bath, and breathe. Breathe the Word of God. It will change your life.

NOTES

_____

_____

_____

_____

_____

_____

_____

TALK

These questions can be used for group discussion or personal reflection.

Question 1

According to 2 Timothy 3:16, how much of Scripture is inspired by God?

_____

_____

_____

_____

Question 2

From the message, what passages of the Bible are criticized for being contradictory? How did Pastor Robert explain the coordination of these two accounts?

_____

_____

_____

_____

Question 3

Read Job 32:8. Who gives understanding and how? When we don't have an understanding of Scripture, what attitude must we have?

_____

_____

_____

_____

Question 4

According to Psalm 33:6, how did God create the heavens and the stars?

_____

_____

_____

_____

Question 5

In Exodus 15:8, we read that God parted the Red Sea, and in
verse 10, He covered the Egyptian army. How did God do this?

_____

_____

_____

_____

PRAY

If studying alone, ask the Holy Spirit to reveal the truth about
Himself to you. If in a group, take some time to pray for each other
as you think about the truths discussed in this session.

EXPLORE

Do you want to go deeper with this teaching? Here are some
additional things to think about, pray for, or write about in your
journal throughout the next week.

Key Quote

> *If Scripture came from the mouth of God, it can't have errors in it. If you deny the inerrancy of Scripture, you will also have to deny the inspiration of Scripture.*

Have you ever doubted the inerrancy of the Bible? How is the Holy Spirit speaking to you about what it means for Scripture to be God-breathed?

_____

_____

_____

_____

_____

Key Verses

Ezekiel 37:1–10; 2 Timothy 3:16; Psalm 33:6; Exodus 15:8–10; Genesis 2:7

What truths stand out to you as you read these verses?

_____

_____

_____

What is the Holy Spirit saying to you through these Scriptures?

_____

_____

_____

Key Question

Read Genesis 2:7. How did God animate humans? How can we receive the breath of God each day?

Key Prayer

Lord, thank You for the understanding, order, strength, and life I receive when I read the Bible. I want to breathe in Your Word each day. Holy Spirit, show me ways to incorporate Scripture into my life every day. In Jesus' name, Amen.

4

DOMINION

Jesus had dominion over all the earth before the Fall, He recovered that dominion on the first Easter. We don't have to wait for the second coming for Jesus to rule.

RECAP

In the previous session, we learned that God breathed life into everything. He inspired—breathed into—the writers of the Bible so that we could have His perfect Word. We should breathe in the Word of God every day.

Did you spend more time reading the Bible this week? What did you read, and what did the Holy Spirit say to you?

ENGAGE

What is your dream vacation destination? Are you actively planning a trip there?

WATCH

Watch "Dominion."

- Look for the things Jesus did to bring dominion.
- Watch for how Jesus' sacrifice and triumph restores our relationship with God.

(If you are not able to watch this teaching on video, read the following. Otherwise, skip to the **Talk** section after viewing.)

READ

Jesus got back dominion of the earth at Easter. Here are a few Scriptures to set up our discussion of the word *dominion*.

When Satan tempted Jesus, he said this to Him in Luke 4:6:

"All this authority I will give You, and their glory; for *this* has been delivered to me, and I give it to whomever I wish."

Delivered means *given over*.

Who gave dominion over to Satan? Adam and Eve did. God originally gave dominion to Adam and Eve:

Then God blessed them, and God said to them, "Be fruitful and multiply; fill the earth and subdue it; have dominion over the fish

of the sea, over the birds of the air, and over every living thing that
moves on the earth" (Genesis 1:28).

Adam and Eve gave dominion over to Satan when they
sinned. Then Satan tells Jesus that he has all the authority—all
the dominion. Jesus doesn't argue with him. But after the resurrection (and before the ascension) Jesus makes this statement:
"All authority has been given to Me in heaven and on earth"
(Matthew 28:18).

We don't have to wait for the second coming to get authority
back. Jesus got it back on the first Easter. Something happened on
the first Easter Day that many haven't seen.

> Let not your heart be troubled; you believe in God, believe also
> in Me. In My Father's house are many mansions; if *it were* not *so,*
> I would have told you. I go to prepare a place for you. (John 14:1-2).

Another word for mansions is dwelling places.

We need to look at this in the context. Jesus is talking to His
disciples, right before the crucifixion. He says I'm going away,
and I'm coming back. But when He spoke about coming back, you
will see that He wasn't talking about the second coming. This is
important to understand so that we can see that we have authority
over sin today.

Consider when it was that Jesus was talking about enabling His
disciples to have a relationship with Him. Was He up in heaven

building mansions so that we would have a place after he came again? Consider instead that He may have been talking about the death and the resurrection. Let's look at John 14:25–29. Jesus is talking about the Holy Spirit and peace:

> These things I have spoken to you while being present with you. But the Helper, the Holy Spirit, whom the Father will send in My name, He will teach you all things, and bring to your remembrance all things that I said to you. Peace I leave with you, My peace I give to you; not as the world gives do I give to you. Let not your heart be troubled, neither let it be afraid. You have heard Me say to you, "I am going away and coming *back* to you." If you loved Me, you would rejoice because I said, "I am going to the Father," for My Father is greater than I.
>
> And now I have told you before it comes, that when it does come to pass, you may believe.

The Holy Spirit and peace are two signs about what's going to happen. Verse 29 is the key for us to know that He is talking about the resurrection and not the second coming. *No one is going to have a problem believing after the second coming.* Every tongue will confess at that time. Jesus is telling His disciples before it happens, so that when it happens, they will believe: *I am going to the Father, and I will get it right so that you can have a relationship with Him* (vv. 1–2). And He's giving two signs: peace and the Holy Spirit. Now look at Chapter 16:16–22:

"A little while, and you will not see Me; and again a little while, and you will see Me, because I go to the Father."

Then *some* of His disciples said among themselves, "What is this that He says to us, 'A little while, and you will not see Me; and again a little while, and you will see Me'; and, 'because I go to the Father'?" They said therefore, "What is this that He says, 'A little while'? We do not know what He is saying."

Now Jesus knew that they desired to ask Him, and He said to them, "Are you inquiring among yourselves about what I said, 'A little while, and you will not see Me; and again a little while, and you will see Me'? Most assuredly, I say to you that you will weep and lament, but the world will rejoice; and you will be sorrowful, but your sorrow will be turned into joy. A woman, when she is in labor, has sorrow because her hour has come; but as soon as she has given birth to the child, she no longer remembers the anguish, for joy that a human being has been born into the world. Therefore you now have sorrow; but I will see you again and your heart will rejoice, and your joy no one will take from you."

"A *little while*, and you won't see me, and again a *little while* and you will see me." Jesus is going to be delivered over to the Pharisees for trial within hours, and then it will be just a few days until He is seen again. It makes a lot more sense that He's talking about the resurrection in three days than the second coming in thousands of years.

The disciples keep asking, "What is a 'little while,'" and Jesus explains that (1) they will weep but the world will rejoice at the first little while, and (2) they will be sorrowful but their sorrow will turn to joy at the second little while. They did not weep when Jesus ascended. They wept when He was crucified. The world rejoiced when He was crucified. The disciples' sorrow was turned to joy at the resurrection. And then He says, "I will see you again." Now we go to resurrection day. In John 20:1 we see that Mary Magdalene sees that the stone is removed from the tomb, which is in the morning. Then we read in verses 11–20:

> But Mary stood outside by the tomb weeping, and as she wept she stooped down *and looked* into the tomb. And she saw two angels in white sitting, one at the head and the other at the feet, where the body of Jesus had lain. Then they said to her, "Woman, why are you weeping?"
>
> She said to them, "Because they have taken away my Lord, and I do not know where they have laid Him."
>
> Now when she had said this, she turned around and saw Jesus standing *there,* and did not know that it was Jesus. Jesus said to her, "Woman, why are you weeping? Whom are you seeking?"
>
> She, supposing Him to be the gardener, said to Him, "Sir, if You have carried Him away, tell me where You have laid Him, and I will take Him away."
>
> Jesus said to her, "Mary!"
>
> She turned and said to Him, "Rabboni!" (which is to say, Teacher).
>
> Jesus said to her, "Do not cling to Me, for I have not yet ascended to My Father; but go to My brethren and say to them, 'I

am ascending to My Father and your Father, and *to* My God and
your God.'"

Mary Magdalene came and told the disciples that she had seen
the Lord, and *that* He had spoken these things to her.

Then, the same day at evening, being the first *day* of the week,
when the doors were shut where the disciples were assembled,
for fear of the Jews, Jesus came and stood in the midst, and said
to them, "Peace *be* with you." When He had said this, He showed
them *His* hands and His side. Then the disciples were glad when
they saw the Lord.

Look how, in verse 14, Mary saw Jesus standing there and
did not know it was Jesus! How strange. She had been traveling
with Jesus for over two years (see John 8:3). There's something
different about His appearance. Then in verse 15 she thinks he is
the *gardener*! This is even stranger. A gardener works in dirt. In the
morning she doesn't recognize Him.

Then Jesus opens her eyes to recognize Him. He tells her not to
touch Him (the word cling here is the same as the word touch, as
when someone touched the hem of His garment) *because He had
not yet ascended to the Father.* This cannot be talking about when He
ascended 40 days later, because He tells Mary to tell the disciples,
"I am ascending to My Father." Present tense. Right now. Ascending
to My Father, and your Father! To My God and to your God.

In verse 19 it is the same day in the evening. Where had Jesus
been all day? Where did He say He was going? He said He was

ascending to the Father. Then Jesus came and said, "Peace be with you" (remember the sign of peace). He showed them His hands and side. That morning He said, "Don't touch Me." Later that same day He says to the disciples, "Touch Me." In verse 20 He showed them His hands and His side. In verse 21, Jesus says, "*Peace* to you! As the Father has sent Me. I also send you." He had been with the Father all day! And He breathed on them and said to *receive the Holy Spirit*.

Jesus had to ascend to the Father and present Himself as an offering so that His disciples could be put into relationship with the Father. Peace and the Holy Spirit are the keys. Now look at Hebrews 9:12:

> Not with the blood of goats and calves, but with His own blood He entered the Most Holy Place once for all, having obtained eternal redemption.

We often miss this verse. But this is when Jesus entered the Most Holy Place—the presence of the Father—and *obtained eternal redemption*.

In Ephesians 4 we read where Jesus first descended into the lower parts of the earth during the three days, then walks up to the devil and says, "Give me the keys. I'm taking it back." He leads "captivity captive" (v. 8). That means He leads the Old Testament saints who were just waiting (they were not in torment) to heaven. While Jesus stops and talks to Mary, the saints go around Jerusalem:

The graves were opened; and many bodies of the saints who had fallen asleep were raised; and coming out of the graves after His resurrection, they went into the holy city and appeared to many (Mathew 27:52–53).

In John 12:31 Jesus says, "Now is the judgment of this world; now the ruler of this world will be cast out." He's saying to the disciples that He's taking it back. Daniel prophesied about this moment in time:

I watched till thrones were put in place,
And the Ancient of Days was seated;
His garment *was* white as snow,
And the hair of His head *was* like pure wool.
His throne *was* a fiery flame,
Its wheels a burning fire;
A fiery stream issued
And came forth from before Him.
A thousand thousands ministered to Him;
Ten thousand times ten thousand stood before Him.
The court was seated,
And the books were opened.
I watched then because of the sound of the pompous words which the horn was speaking; I watched till the beast was slain, and its body destroyed and given to the burning flame. As for the rest of the beasts, they had their dominion taken away, yet their lives were prolonged for a season and a time.

I was watching in the night visions,
And behold, *One* like the Son of Man,
Coming with the clouds of heaven!
He came to the Ancient of Days,
And they brought Him near before Him.
Then to Him was given dominion and glory and a kingdom,
That all peoples, nations, and languages should serve Him.
His dominion *is* an everlasting dominion,
Which shall not pass away,
And His kingdom *the one*
Which shall not be destroyed. (Daniel 7:9–14).

What a glorious image of the Father! This is not the same beast as in Revelation. There are four beasts, and this is the first beast to be destroyed. That is sin. *Sin* was destroyed at the resurrection. Romans 6:14 says, "Sin shall not have dominion over you." The opening of the books here is not the judgment of Revelation. It is the judgment of sin.

In verse 12 Jesus explains that the beasts' *dominion* was taken away, but their lives were prolonged for a season. Satan's dominion was taken away two thousand years ago. His life was prolonged for a season, but he has no more *dominion*!

Verse 7:13 describes Jesus, the Son of Man, coming to the Father with the clouds of heaven: with the Old Testament saints. Hebrews 12:1 calls them a "great cloud of witnesses." And verse 14 describes the transfer of dominion to Jesus: an everlasting dominion that shall never be destroyed.

Daniel summarizes this in verses 21-22:

I was watching; and the same horn was making war against the saints, and prevailing against them, until the Ancient of Days came, and a judgment was made *in favor* of the saints of the Most High, and the time came for the saints to possess the kingdom.

Here's what happened. Two thousand years ago, the Ancient of Days—the Judge—walked in. He looked at Satan on one side ... He looked at the saints on the other side. Then He looked at the bloody, bruised, battered, and beaten body of His Son, and He said, [pounding the gavel] "Satan, you lose. Saints, you win!" That's what happened on Easter.

Satan doesn't have dominion over you anymore, and we don't have to wait until the second coming. Because of the resurrection, we get it now.

Jesus went away so we can have relationship with the Father.
Jesus ascended on resurrection day.
It was finished on resurrection day.

NOTES

_____

_____

_____

_____

_____

_____

TALK

These questions can be used for group discussion or personal reflection.

Question 1

Read John 20:14-15. Why is it important that Mary didn't recognize Jesus when she saw Him earlier in the day? Did the disciples recognize Him later in the day?

_____

_____

_____

_____

Question 2

Hebrews 9:12 says that when He entered the Most Holy Place, Jesus obtained eternal redemption for us with His blood. How does that eternal redemption affect our here and now?

_____

_____

_____

_____

Question 3

Read Matthew 27:52–53. Just for fun, take a few minutes and talk about what it must have looked like around Jerusalem that day. What do you think the people living in that day must have thought and felt? Did they know the significance?

_____

_____

_____

_____

Question 4

Read Daniel 7:9–14. If Satan has already been slain and dominion has been given to Jesus, how does that change the way we live now?

_____

_____

_____

_____

PRAY

If studying alone, ask the Holy Spirit to reveal the truth about Himself to you. If in a group, take some time to pray for each other as you think about the truths discussed in this session.

EXPLORE

Do you want to go deeper with this teaching? Here are some additional things to think about, pray for, or write about in your journal throughout the next week.

Key Quote

Satan doesn't have dominion over you anymore, and we don't have to wait until the second coming. Because of the resurrection, we get it now.

What does it mean to you personally that we get to have a relationship with the Father now as a result of what Jesus did?

_____

_____

_____

_____

_____

Key Verses

Luke 4:6; Genesis 1:28; Matthew 27:52-53; 28:18; John 12:31; 14:1-2, 25-29; 16:16-22, 20:1, 11-22; Hebrews 9:12; Daniel 7:9-14, 21-22; Romans 6:14; Colossians 2:15

What truths stand out to you as you read these verses?

_____

_____

_____

What is the Holy Spirit saying to you through these Scriptures?

_____

_____

_____

Key Question

Now that our relationship with the Father has been restored, how does this change our everyday lives?

Key Prayer

Jesus, You finished it all. Thank You for dying for us and taking *all* of the punishment of sin on Your head so we can be restored to our Father and Your Father. Help us to become more aware of our relationship with the Father and with the impact that has on our lives every day. We acknowledge Your dominion over our lives, and we ask You to help us walk in the truth of what You did for us. In Jesus' name, Amen.

5

SYMBOLS

God uses symbols throughout the Bible to give us greater understanding and revelation of His ways. We must value God's Word and make time for reading it every day.

RECAP

In the previous session, we learned that the Bible is a love story in which God rescued us and gave us redemption from sin. Now we are called to a purpose, which is to help bring His kingdom down to earth and rescue others.

What insight did you have about your mission or purpose in life this past week?

ENGAGE

What is your favorite summer memory as a kid, and why is this memory special?

WATCH

Watch "Symbols."

- Look for the many spiritual symbols throughout the Bible.
- Watch for the ways God uses symbols to help us combat the enemy and fulfill the mission of the Church.

(If you are not able to watch this teaching on video, read the following. Otherwise, skip to the **Talk** section after viewing.)

READ

As we continue this series "More than Words," remember that I said the next attack is going to come against the Bible. Because if the Bible is not God's Word, then man can be god. Man can have the final say. The month after I said this, GQ Magazine put out a list of the 21 books you don't need to read—and they put the Bible on the list. They also put Mark Twain's books on there, as well as *The Old Man and the Sea* and *Lonesome Dove*. Also *Lord of the Rings* and *Gulliver's Travels*. I wouldn't put too much stock in the literary selections of a fashion magazine. But you can see the attack is real.

The Bible is more than words. The Bible is not of anyone's own personal interpretation. The method of Bible interpretation is called exegesis. The Greek words mean to "call out," like drawing water out of a well. The opposite of exegesis is eisegesis, which means to read a meaning into. That is what is often happening today. People are reading their own meaning of Scripture "into."

There are several forms of exegesis. The most important is cohesive exegesis, which means that it has to be cohesive with the entire Bible and the nature and the character of God.

We have a tendency to believe that we are humans having a spiritual experience. But the truth is we are spirits having a human experience. We're spirits. The Bible is a spiritual book, written by a spiritual being, to spiritual beings. That's why GQ magazine doesn't have a clue. The Bible says that the natural man can't even understand this book.

The Bible Is Full of Spiritual Symbols

We will be going through a lot of Scripture, and we won't have time to exegete all the passages. I hope you will take time to listen and then go back and read them.

> The people asked, and He brought quail,
> And satisfied them with the bread of heaven.
> He opened the rock, and water gushed out (Psalm 105:40-41).

I talked about bread and water earlier in this series. Remember that the Bible interprets itself. First Corinthians 10:1-4 shows that these are *spiritual* symbols:

> I do not want you to be unaware that all our fathers were under
> the cloud, all passed through the sea, all were baptized into Moses
> in the cloud and in the sea, all ate the same spiritual food, and all
> drank the same spiritual drink. For they drank of that spiritual Rock
> that followed them, and that Rock was Christ.

Bread, the water, and the rock represent Jesus. They are spiritual symbols.

Revelation 11:8 says, "And their dead bodies *will lie* in the street of the great city which spiritually is called Sodom and Egypt, where also our Lord was crucified." Spiritually, he says, there is a name for it.

We see numerous symbols in Luke chapter 10:

> Then the seventy returned with joy, saying, "Lord, even the demons
> are subject to us in Your name."
>
> And He said to them, "I saw Satan fall like lightning from
> heaven. Behold, I give you the authority to trample on serpents and
> scorpions, and over all the power of the enemy, and nothing shall
> by any means hurt you. Nevertheless do not rejoice in this, that the
> spirits are subject to you, but rather rejoice because your names are
> written in heaven" (vv. 17–20).

Before serpents and scorpions, we see demons and Satan. After serpents and scorpions, we see the enemy and spirits. Look how clearly Jesus describes these symbols. Jesus is not talking about snakes and stinging creatures. He is talking about demons, evil spirits, Satan, the enemy. That's the context. Remember, one Person authored the Bible. So if serpents and scorpions represent demons in Luke, they represent the same thing in Revelation, Genesis, Ezekiel, and Jeremiah.

Jesus is taking about authority over demons. In verse 21 He thanks the Father for hiding these things from the "wise and prudent" and revealing them to "baby" believers. Read the book of Revelation in context with the rest of the Bible.

Revelation 9:3-4 says, "Then out of the smoke locusts came upon the earth. And to them was given power, as the scorpions of the earth have power. They were commanded not to harm the grass of the earth, or any green thing, or any tree, but only those men who do not have the seal of God on their foreheads." We know that scorpions are from Luke. Locusts have the same power. This passage says that the locusts here will not be able to harm *green* things. *Green* trees. Psalm 1 says that a man who meditates on the Word is like a *tree planted* by the water. When the demonic spirits are released in the end times, they *will* be able to harm men who do not have the seal of God on their forehead, but they *can't* harm men who meditate on the Word of God.

We should read the Bible every day and read it in context.

Sheep Have an Enemy

Sheep represent something. Psalm 100:3 says, "We are His people and the sheep of His pasture." We are called sheep. We believe in that symbol. Look at Ezekiel 34:1-2:

And the word of the Lord came to me, saying, "Son of man, prophesy against the shepherds of Israel, prophesy and say to them, 'Thus says the Lord God to the shepherds: "Woe to the shepherds of Israel who feed themselves! Should not the shepherds feed the flocks?"'"

Ezekiel is not talking about literal shepherds. He's talking about pastors; spiritual leaders. Woe to them if they do not feed the flocks. There is another symbol in the spiritual language: In Ezekiel 34:5, the sheep became food for the "beasts of the field." Beasts of the field doesn't mean lions and tigers. They mean demonic spirits. It represents the enemy.

Genesis 3:1 begins "Now the serpent," which we already believe is Satan. But we also know this from Revelation 12:9, which specifically calls the serpent Satan.

Back to beasts of the field. The serpent represents Satan. Now here is the full text of Genesis 3:1: "Now the serpent was more cunning than any beast of the field which the Lord God had made." Satan is the most cunning of the fallen angels: the beasts of the field.

Satan was with Jesus for the full 40 days in the wilderness. In Mark 1:13 we see that Satan took the beasts of the field with him when he tempted Jesus.

Mark 4:2 says Jesus taught by parables. Jesus also said in John 5:19 that He never does anything unless He sees the Father do it first. When did Jesus first see the Father speak in parables?

In the Old Testament. In Ezekiel God was talking about the king of Egypt and Babylon. He said that He was going to break Pharaoh's arms. God didn't break his literal arms. He broke his strength. He was speaking in a parable. God says in Psalm 78:2 that He speaks in parables.

In Mark 4:2-4 we see the birds of the air used as the same kind of symbol. They devoured the seed that had been sowed (the seed is the Word). Satan and his army took away the words that had been sown in the disciples' hearts.

He talks about the beasts of the field and birds of the air so we are not naive about the schemes of the enemy. He wants to give us wisdom through the Bible so that we are empowered to resist the enemy.

God Has a Plan

Now look at Daniel 4:10-15:

These *were* the visions of my head *while* on my bed:
I was looking, and behold,
A tree in the midst of the earth,
And its height was great.
The tree grew and became strong;
Its height reached to the heavens,
And it could be seen to the ends of all the earth.
Its leaves *were* lovely,
Its fruit abundant,

And in it *was* food for all.
The beasts of the field found shade under it,
The birds of the heavens dwelt in its branches,
And all flesh was fed from it.

I saw in the visions of my head *while* on my bed, and there was a watcher, a holy one, coming down from heaven. He cried aloud and said thus:
"Chop down the tree and cut off its branches,
Strip off its leaves and scatter its fruit.
Let the beasts get out from under it,
And the birds from its branches.
Nevertheless leave the stump and roots in the earth,
Bound with a band of iron and bronze,
In the tender grass of the field.
Let it be wet with the dew of heaven,
And *let* him graze with the beasts
On the grass of the earth."

Babylon represents a mixture of the Church and the world. When Israel left Babylon after captivity, only 10% left. In this passage, the tree is the Church. In Isaiah 6:13, after God tells Isaiah that he will preach to a rebellious people who will not believe, God says that when the tree is cut down, "the holy seed shall be its stump." In other words, they are the true believers—the remnant that will be left when God brings judgment on the worldly church.

Note also that the birds nest in the branches (John 15:5). We are the branches.

Matthew 12:43–44 says that demonic spirits returned to the man's house (his spirit) because it was "swept clean." It was empty. He didn't fill it with Jesus, the Holy Spirit, and the Word of God. Those who don't remain committed to God will suffer the same fate. We need to drive the enemies out of the land.

Deuteronomy 7:22 has the last symbol: "And the Lord your God will drive out those nations before you little by little; you will be unable to destroy them at once, lest the beasts of the field become *too* numerous for you." We need to keep reading, growing, and walking with God, because we've got to drive the beasts of the field and the birds of the air out of our land. We must stay connected to the vine of Christ. When we do, we will be like "trees planted by streams of living water." Jesus is the living water.

NOTES

_____

_____

_____

_____

_____

_____

TALK

These questions can be used for group discussion or personal reflection.

Question 1
Have you ever felt like the Bible was confusing or overwhelming to understand? Why?

_____

_____

_____

_____

Question 2
Pastor Robert shared that many of today's intellectuals believe that the Bible isn't relevant. Do you agree or disagree with this notion?

_____

_____

_____

_____

Question 3

What has been your experience with the Bible? Is the Bible significant in your life?

_____

_____

_____

_____

Question 4

Do you believe that God speaks to us personally through the Bible? Why or why not.?

_____

_____

_____

_____

Question 5

Read Mark 4:2-9. What do the symbols in this passage represent? Now read Mark 4:13-15. What surprises you about this parable?

_____

_____

_____

_____

PRAY

If studying alone, ask the Holy Spirit to reveal the truth about Himself to you. If in a group, take some time to pray for each other as you think about the truths discussed in this session.

EXPLORE

Do you want to go deeper with this teaching? Here are some additional things to think about, pray for, or write about in your journal throughout the next week:

Key Quote

> The Bible is a spiritual book, written by a spiritual being, to spiritual beings.

Do you set aside time to study the Bible every day? If not, how could you adjust your schedule to make the time?

_____

_____

_____

_____

_____

Key Verses

Mark 4:2-9; Psalm 105:40-41; 1 Corinthians 10:1-4; Ezekiel 34:1-2;
Daniel 4:10-15

What truths stand out to you as you read these verses?

_____

_____

_____

What is the Holy Spirit saying to you through these Scriptures?

_____

_____

_____

Key Question

Can you share a time or experience when God spoke to you and
directed you through the Bible?

Key Prayer

Heavenly Father, thank You for giving us the most sacrificial
offering of all—Your Son, Jesus. Thank You for giving us the gift
of the Your Word. Help us to study it and understand what You
are saying. We want to follow You every day of our lives. In Jesus'
name, Amen.

6

SIGHT

When we cannot see or hear, we miss out on the heart of God's Word. We need to set aside pride and repent in order for us to receive the spiritual revelation God has for us.

RECAP

In the previous session, we learned about the many symbols used throughout the Bible and how understanding those symbols gives us greater revelation of God's Word and His plan for us.

What insights about God did you experience this week that was aided by a spiritual symbol?

ENGAGE

Besides Jesus, which person in the Bible intrigues you the most? Why?

WATCH

Watch "Sight."

- Look for the causes and effects of spiritual blindness.
- Watch for how our eyes can be opened and sight restored.

(If you are not able to watch this teaching on video, read the following. Otherwise, skip to the **Talk** section after viewing.)

READ

Spiritual blindness is a real disease. It takes spiritual eyes to understand the Bible.

Spiritual Blindness Steals Our Understanding

You will not understand the Bible if you are spiritually blind. The Bible talks a lot about this. As we did with spiritual symbols, we must look at these scriptures allegorically.

> Hear, you deaf;
> And look, you blind, that you may see.
> Who *is* blind but My servant,
> Or deaf as My messenger *whom* I send?
> Who *is* blind as *he who is* perfect,
> And blind as the Lord's servant?

Seeing many things, but you do not observe;
Opening the ears, but he does not hear. (Isaiah 42:18-20).

Jesus is clearly not talking about those who are physically deaf or blind. See also Isaiah 42:20, Jeremiah 5:21, Ezekiel 12:2, and Zephaniah 1:17. Rebellion and sin are other causes of spiritual blindness.

In Matthew 13:14-15 we see the progression:

And in them the prophecy of Isaiah is fulfilled, which says:
"Hearing you will hear and shall not understand,
And seeing you will see and not perceive;
For the hearts of this people have grown dull.
Their ears are hard of hearing,
And their eyes they have closed,
Lest they should see with *their* eyes and hear with *their* ears,
Lest they should understand with *their* hearts and turn,
So that I should heal them."

They hear but don't understand, and they see without perceiving, because their hearts have grown dull. See the progression. They have to be able to see with their spiritual eyes and ears so they can understand God's Word, so that they can turn, and He can heal them. The reason many people are not spiritually healed is because they don't turn from their sin. The reason they don't turn from their sin is because they don't understand what it's doing to them. The reason they don't understand what it's doing to them is that they are spiritually blind and deaf. Spiritual blindness causes you to be physically, mentally, spiritually, and emotionally sick.

God's Word is the only thing that heals us. Even in the natural we can be looking at something and not see it. You might read a chapter of the Bible and not understand it. You can be looking at someone and not see them, because your mind is somewhere else.

Pride Causes Spiritual Blindness

The only reason we would be rebellious or continue to sin is because of pride.

Jesus healed a man who was blind from birth, which had never been done before, and the Pharisees were angry about it. They were mad at Jesus. Here is what Jesus said:

> "For judgment I have come into this world, that those who do not see may see, and that those who see may be made blind."
> Then *some* of the Pharisees who were with Him heard these words, and said to Him, "Are we blind also?"
> Jesus said to them, "If you were blind, you would have no sin; but now you say, 'We see.' Therefore your sin remains" (John 9:39-41).

Because the Pharisees said they could see, their sin remained. If they were truly blind, they would not have sinned. Remember what happened when Paul was saved? Ananias prayed for him, and scales fell off his eyes! Think about that.

Jesus said that He came into this world so that the spiritually blind would be able to see. "And those of you who say you can see, without Me—that you don't need Me—you'll just be made blind." So yes, Jesus said, you are blind. But if they would admit that they couldn't see without Him, they would have no sin; Jesus would forgive all their sin.

Here are a couple of other Scriptures that we must look at allegorically:

And in that day seven women shall take hold of one man, saying,
"We will eat our own food and wear our own apparel;
Only let us be called by your name,
To take away our reproach" (Isaiah 4:1).

In Revelation there are seven churches. Churches are often called women in the Bible. The Church is the bride of Christ. Those seven churches of Asia Minor represent the end time Church. This verse says that in those days the end times Church will take hold of one new man, which is Jesus. But they will want to have their own teaching (food) and their own righteousness (apparel) and be called by His name so they would look to be without reproach.

When I have cut off your supply of bread, ten women shall bake your bread in one oven, and they shall bring back your

bread by weight, and you shall eat and not be satisfied.
(Leviticus 26:26).

I believe this means, allegorically, that Jesus is saying, "When you turn away from Me, I'm going to cut off your supply of bread. When I cut it off, 10 different churches are going to prepare their teaching in one city. They're going to prepare a little Sunday School book in one place and bring it back in portions of just a few verses ... and you're not going to be satisfied."

Jesus' Opens Blind Eyes

Look at Mark 8:23-25:

So He took the blind man by the hand and led him out of the town. And when He had spit on his eyes and put His hands on him, He asked him if he saw anything.

And he looked up and said, "I see men like trees, walking."

Then He put *His* hands on his eyes again and made him look up. And he was restored and saw everyone clearly.

I once heard a television preacher says, "You see, even with Jesus, it doesn't always work the first time." I couldn't believe it. That couldn't be right. I remember thinking, "Lord, I'm going to figure this out." There must be something else here. I read everything I could think of. Three hours later I couldn't understand. Then the Lord came to me and said, "Do you think I know what that means?" I said of course, and the Lord said, "Then why don't you just ask?" The moment I began to ask, the Lord downloaded it to me.

The man said, "I see men like trees walking." Think about the symbols of the Bible. Psalm 1:1-3 calls a man who meditates on the Word a tree. Psalm 52:8 reads, "I am like a green olive tree in the house of God." Psalm 92:12, Jeremiah 17:7-8, and Isaiah 55:12 all speak about trees in the sense of *people*. Matthew 7:17 talks about trees bearing fruit. Jesus called people trees. Zechariah refers to the two anointed ones in Revelation as olive trees.

It's quite simple. When Jesus put his hands on the man the first time, he opened his spiritual eyes. When He put His hands on him the second time, He opened his natural eyes.

Immediately before this, in verses 13-21, the disciples could not comprehend what Jesus meant when He said to beware of the leaven of the Pharisees. They thought He was worried because they only had one loaf of bread with them. He had just fed 5,000 people with five loaves and 4,000 people with seven loaves, but they were still so spiritually blind they couldn't understand! Jesus was referring to the leaders' false teaching. Jesus said, "How is it you do not understand?" (v. 21). If He wanted bread, He could just whip some up! Bread was not the problem. He was talking about something in the spiritual realm, and they had eyes, but they could not see.

If you don't read the Bible with spiritual eyes, you can't understand it. If you can't understand it, you won't turn from what is keeping you from getting healed,

NOTES

_____

_____

_____

_____

_____

_____

TALK

These questions can be used for group discussion or personal reflection.

Question 1

What are two things that contribute to spiritual blindness (Ezekiel 12:2; Zephaniah 1:17)?

_____

_____

_____

_____

Question 2
Read Matthew 13:15. What must happen before our eyes and ears are spiritually attuned to God and we are healed?

_____

_____

_____

_____

Question 3
Referencing Mark 8:22–25, what does this statement mean: "The first time Jesus opened the man's spiritual eyes; the second time his natural eyes were opened."?

_____

_____

_____

_____

Question 4
Read Psalm 1:3, 52:8, and Jeremiah 17:8. What do trees symbolize in these verses? Describe the two types of trees mentioned in Matthew 7:17.

_____

_____

_____

_____

Question 5
Read Mark 8:13-21. What was Jesus specifically warning His
disciples about regarding "the leaven of the Pharisees and the
leaven of Herod"? Why did the disciples not understand what Jesus
was trying to teach them?

_____

_____

_____

_____

PRAY

If studying alone, ask the Holy Spirit to reveal the truth about
Himself to you. If in a group, take some time to pray for each other
as you think about the truths discussed in this session.

EXPLORE

Do you want to go deeper with this teaching? Here are some
additional things to think about, pray for, or write about in your
journal throughout the next week.

Key Quote

> *The reason many people are not spiritually healed is because they*
> *don't turn from their sin. The reason they don't turn from their sin is*
> *because they don't understand what it's doing to them. The reason*
> *they don't understand what it's doing to them is that they are*
> *spiritually blind and deaf.*

What are some examples of how you can read the Bible with spiritually blind eyes?

_____

_____

_____

_____

_____

Key Verses

Isaiah 42:18-20; John 9:39-41; Mark 8:13-21

What truths stand out to you as you read these verses?

_____

_____

_____

What is the Holy Spirit saying to you through these Scriptures?

_____

_____

_____

Key Question

Is there is an area of your life where you may be spiritually deaf or blind? If so, ask God to open your eyes and ears to the revelation of His Word.

Key Prayer

Dear God, I repent of sinfulness and pride; please forgive me. I come to You as a child, confessing that I cannot understand Your Word without guidance from You. I receive Your help now. In Jesus' name, Amen.

7

LIGHT

When we are in a dark place, God's Word dispels the darkness and
brings us back into the light.

RECAP

In the previous session, we learned about the dangers of spiritual blindness. We overcome spiritual blindness by conquering our pride, repenting of sin, and opening our hearts to God's Word.

Did you see some area of your life where you were spiritually blind this week? If so, how did you overcome it? Did you look at the Bible differently?

ENGAGE

Have you ever gone camping? What was your favorite (or least favorite) part of the experience?

WATCH

Watch "Light."

- Look for the things that light does for us.
- Watch for how we learn which direction or steps to take.

(If you are not able to watch this teaching on video, read the following. Otherwise, skip to the **Talk** section after viewing.)

READ

God's Word is light.

> Your word *is* a lamp to my feet
> And a light to my path (Psalm 119:105).

This short and well-known verse says a great deal about God's Word. His Word is a lamp to my feet so I'll know where to take the next step, and a light to my path so I'll know what direction God wants me to take.

Light Dispels Darkness

I'm sure every one of you at some time has walked across a dark room in the middle of the night and stubbed your toe. You're not clumsy. You just needed some light. Think of the analogy. We should be walking in the Spirit, but we're living in a dark world. So how many Christians are stumbling spiritually because they are not using their lamp?

Light takes away darkness. There is no struggle between light and darkness. We are in a struggle, but God is not in a struggle with darkness. When you enter a room and turn on the light, the darkness leaves immediately.

John 3:20 says, "Everyone practicing evil hates the light and does not come to the light, lest his deeds should be exposed." When we used to have film cameras, if a light was turned on accidentally before it was processed, it would expose the film and the image would immediately go away. So if you've taken pictures of dark things, perhaps immoral things, expose it to the light. It will ruin that film.

Jesus talks about this in Luke 11:

No one, when he has lit a lamp, puts *it* in a secret place or under a basket, but on a lampstand, that those who come in may see the light. The lamp of the body is the eye. Therefore, when your eye is good, your whole body also is full of light. But when *your eye* is bad, your body also *is* full of darkness. Therefore take heed that the light which is in you is not darkness. If then your whole body *is* full of light, having no part dark, *the* whole *body* will be full of light, as when the bright shining of a lamp gives you light (vv. 33-36).

Think about how much darkness our eyes see every day. I opened up Yahoo the other day to look at how many of the articles were either about murder or immorality. I got so discouraged I stopped counting. We've got all these articles about darkness. We spend hours reading about darkness. Can you imagine how much better it would be if we spent that many hours letting light in?

Light gets into the body through the eye—what you see. I counseled a man who was struggling with lust, with all the images that he had in his mind. He said he really wanted to get help. So I told him to spend 30 minutes every day reading the Bible. I told him to start in Matthew. He did that. He came back a month later and said it's amazing how much lust had been driven out of his mind, and he was thinking more about God and godly things. A few months later he and his wife went to a "chick-flick" that had one inappropriate scene in it. He told me that what used to attract him now repulsed him. He was repulsed at that scene because of the light that was in him. Light dispels darkness.

Light Recovers Lost Things

If you lose something, you get a light so you can find it. It's obvious. Jesus tells this story about someone who lost something. This story comes between the story of the lost sheep and the prodigal son. All these stories talk about people.

> What woman, having ten silver coins, if she loses one coin, does not light a lamp, sweep the house, and search carefully until she finds *it?* And when she has found *it,* she calls *her* friends and neighbors together, saying, "Rejoice with me, for I have found the piece which

I lost!" Likewise, I say to you, there is joy in the presence of the angels of God over one sinner who repents (Luke 15:8-10).

What if you lose your job? What if you lose your relationship? What if you lose an investment? What if you lose your integrity ... your reputation, by doing something you never thought you would do? Anytime you lose something, light a lamp. Read the Bible. Ask God for the light of revelation if you become lost.

Let's talk about people. When children grow older, there is a natural progression where you begin to lose some of the control that you had over that child. You have to hope the child makes good decisions on their own. One important time is when your child is considering getting married. We asked each of our kids if we could speak into their life about this and made a covenant with them to help them walk in this decision.

Our son James was pursued by girls, though James never pursued them. There was as girl in high school that pursued him— she was a Christian, and a nice girl, but I didn't think she was right for him or that the time was right.

I asked the Lord for guidance, and one day God spoke to me in my daily Bible reading about fasting. I decided to fast from meat for 40 days. I realized that fasting helps us pull back from the world to help us hear God. I asked James and this girl to fast from each other for 40 days. No contact of any kind for 40 days.

Hebrews 4:12 speaks of dividing between soul and spirit. The soul includes the mind, will, and emotions. Our will considers our thoughts and emotions as it makes decisions. The Word separates what we think is right from the spirit—what *is* right.

They agreed to fast for 40 days, but on Saturday she called him. He picked up the phone from the middle of a nap, and when he realized who it was, he said they shouldn't be talking. She said that what your father doesn't know won't hurt him. And he said, "Goodbye." Then he told me that was the end of the relationship. He said, "If she won't respect you, she won't respect me either."

Light Shows the Way

We all have decisions we need to make—about jobs, college, relationships, and so forth. The Bible talks about general and specific revelation. For example, the general revelation of God is, *How* do you marry? The specific revelation of God is, *Whom* do you marry? God can give you specific revelation. He can speak through the Bible. I'm going to show you how to get a word from God through God's Word. There are three steps: *Praise. Prayer. Proclaim.*

Enter God's presence with *praise*. Psalm 100:4. Worship.

Pray about what you need to pray about. Write your prayers. What's on your heart.

Proclaim means to read God's Word. If you are praying about marriage, think about any stories that deal with marriage. Abraham and Sarah. Isaac and Rebekah. Boaz and Ruth. Jesus and the Church.

Remember that as you read the Bible, you need to exegete. The Old Testament generally has allegorical principles, and the New Testament has applicable principles. For example, Sarah called

Abraham "Lord." That's allegorical. You don't have to call your husband "Lord." The application is that you should respect your husband.

A lot of people think that their pastor or parent or someone else should hear from God. But we all have our own personal relationship with God. When you have a decision, just praise, pray, and proclaim.

NOTES

_____

_____

_____

_____

_____

_____

TALK

These questions can be used for group discussion or personal reflection.

Question 1

Psalm 18:28 reads, "For You will light my lamp; the Lord my God will enlighten my darkness." Has God ever touched your life in this way? How has your experience brought light to someone else going through a similar circumstance?

_____

_____

_____

_____

Question 2

Read Luke 11:33–36. In what ways can darkness infiltrate our thoughts and lives? How can light transform our thoughts and lives?

_____

_____

_____

_____

Question 3

What does it mean when Pastor Robert says, "We are in a war with darkness, but God is not"?

_____

_____

_____

_____

Question 4

Luke 15:8-10 speaks about a woman who lost, then found her coin. Have you ever lost something that God returned? (Examples: a relationship, an investment, health, or other loss.) If you feel comfortable doing so, please share how God turned this problem around.

_____

_____

_____

_____

PRAY

If studying alone, ask the Holy Spirit to reveal the truth about Himself to you. If in a group, take some time to pray for each other as you think about the truths discussed in this session.

EXPLORE

Do you want to go deeper with this teaching? Here are some additional things to think about, pray for, or write about in your journal throughout the next week:

Key Quote

> *What if you lose your job? What if you lose your relationship? What if you lose an investment? What if you lose your integrity ... your reputation? ... Anytime you lose something, light a lamp.*

Have you ever "lit a lamp" by going to the Word when you lost something? How did God direct your path?

_____

_____

_____

_____

_____

Key Verses

Luke 11 and 15

What truths stand out to you as you read these verses?

_____

_____

_____

What is the Holy Spirit saying to you through these Scriptures?

_____

_____

_____

Key Question

How do the three "Ps" (*praise, prayer, and proclamation*) work to get a word from God for you?

Key Prayer

Dear God, please help me by bringing Your light into my situation. I need understanding and direction. I cannot solve this problem by myself. In Jesus' name, Amen.

LEADER'S GUIDE

The *More than Words* Leader's Guide is designed to help you lead your small group or class through the *More than Words* curriculum. Use this guide along with the curriculum for a life-changing, interactive experience.

BEFORE YOU MEET

- Ask God to prepare the hearts and minds of the people in your group. Ask Him to show you how to encourage each person to integrate the principles all of you discover into your daily lives through group discussion and writing in your journals.
- Preview the video segment for the week.
- Plan how much time you'll give to each portion of your meeting (see the suggested schedule below). In case you're unable to get through all of the activities in the time you have planned, here is a list of the most important questions (from the **Talk** section) for each week.

SUGGESTED SCHEDULE FOR THE GROUP:

1. **Engage** and **Recap** (5 Minutes)
2. **Watch** and **Read** (20 Minutes)
3. **Talk** (25 Minutes)
4. **Pray** (10 minutes)

SESSION ONE

Q: In the Old Testament, God sent manna on a daily basis. Why is it important to have a daily routine of reading the Bible? How does it affect us when we do *and* when we don't have our "daily bread"?

Q: What are some practical ways to memorize Scripture and apply it to our lives?

SESSION TWO

Q: How are we cleansed? Read Ephesians 5:25-26. When we allow this to happen, how does this affect our thoughts?

Q: Sometimes, we overwhelm ourselves with words. How did Jesus deal with a flood of words from Satan?

SESSION THREE

Q: Read Job 32:8. Who gives understanding and how? When we don't have an understanding of Scripture, what attitude must we have?

Q: Read Genesis 2:7. How did God animate humans? How can we receive the breath of God each day?

SESSION FOUR

Q: Hebrews 9:12 says that when He entered the Most Holy Place Jesus obtained eternal redemption for us with His blood. How does that eternal redemption affect our here and now?

Q: What does it mean to you personally that we get to have a relationship with the Father now as a result of what Jesus did?

SESSION FIVE

Q: What has been your experience with the Bible? Is the Bible significant in your life? Share.

Q: Do you set aside time to study the Bible every day? If not, how could you adjust your schedule to make the time?

SESSION SIX

Q: Read Matthew 13:15. What must happen before our eyes and ears are spiritually attuned to God or we are healed?

Q: What are some examples of how you can read the Bible with spiritually blind eyes?

SESSION SEVEN

Q: Read Luke 11:33-36. In what ways can darkness infiltrate our thoughts and lives? How can light transform our thoughts and lives?

Q: How do the three "Ps" (*praise, prayer, and proclamation*) work to get a word from God for you?

HOW TO USE THE CURRICULUM:

This study has a simple design.
Each week:

The One Thing:
This is a brief statement under each session title that sums up the main point—the key idea—of the session.

Recap:
Recap the previous week's session, inviting members to share about any opportunities they have encountered throughout the week that apply what they learned (this doesn't apply to the first week).

Engage:
Ask the icebreaker question to help get people talking and feeling comfortable with one another.

Watch:
Watch the videos (recommended).

Read:
If you're unable to watch the videos, read these sections.

Talk:
The questions in these lessons are intentionally open-ended. Use them to help the group members reflect on Scripture and the lesson.

Pray:
Ask members to share their concerns and then pray together. Be sensitive to the Holy Spirit and the needs of the group.

Explore:
Encourage members to complete the written portion in their books before the next meeting.

KEY TIPS FOR THE LEADER:

- Generate participation and discussion.
- Resist the urge to teach. The goal is for great conversation that leads to discovery.
- Ask open-ended questions—questions that can't be answered with "yes" or "no" (e.g., "What do you think about that?" rather than "Do you agree?")

- When a question arises, ask the group for their input instead of answering it yourself before allowing anyone else to respond.
- Be comfortable with silence. If you ask a question and no one responds, rephrase the question and wait for a response. Your primary role is to create an environment where people feel comfortable to be themselves and participate, not to provide the answers to all of their questions.
- Ask the group to pray for each other from week to week, especially about key issues that arise during your group time. This is how you begin to build authentic community and encourage spiritual growth within the group.

KEYS TO A DYNAMIC SMALL GROUP:

Relationships
Meaningful, encouraging relationships are the foundation of a dynamic small group. Teaching, discussion, worship, and prayer are important elements of a group meeting, but the depth of each element is often dependent upon the depth of the relationships between members.

Availability
Building a sense of community within your group requires members to prioritize their relationships with one another. This means being available to listen, care for one another, and meet each other's needs.

Mutual Respect

Mutual respect is shown when members value each other's opinions (even when they disagree) and are careful never to put down or embarrass others in the group (including their spouses, who may or may not be present).

Openness

A healthy small group environment encourages sincerity and transparency. Members treat each other with grace in areas of weakness, allowing each other room to grow.

Confidentiality

To develop authenticity and a sense of safety within the group, each member must be able to trust that things discussed within the group will not be shared outside the group.

Shared Responsibility

Group members will share the responsibility of group meetings by using their God-given abilities to serve at each gathering. Some may greet, some may host, some may teach, etc. Ideally, each person should be available to care for others as needed.

Sensitivity

Dynamic small groups are born when the leader consistently seeks and is responsive to the guidance of the Holy Spirit, following His leading throughout the meeting as opposed to sticking to the "agenda." This guidance is especially important during the discussion and ministry time.

Fun!

Dynamic small groups take the time to have fun! Create an atmosphere for fun, and be willing to laugh at yourself every now and then!

ABOUT THE AUTHOR

Robert Morris is the lead senior pastor of Gateway Church, a multicampus church in the Dallas/ Fort Worth Metroplex. Since it began in 2000, the church has grown to more than 39,000 active members. His television program is aired in over 190 countries, and his radio feature, *Worship & the Word with Pastor Robert,* airs on radio stations across America. He serves as chancellor of The King's University and is the bestselling author of 15 books including *The Blessed Life, Truly Free, Frequency*, and *Beyond Blessed*. Robert and his wife, Debbie, have been married 38 years and are blessed with one married daughter, two married sons, and nine grandchildren. He lives in Dallas, TX.

More resources for your small group by Pastor Robert Morris!

tudy Guide: 978-1-945529-54-2
DVD: 978-1-949399-41-7

Study Guide: 978-1-949399-54-7
DVD: 978-1-949399-51-6

Study Guide: 978-1-945529-51-1
DVD: 978-1-949399-49-3

Study Guide: 978-1-945529-71-9
DVD: 978-1-949399-50-9

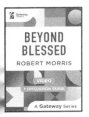

DVD + Discussion Guide:
978-1-949399-68-4

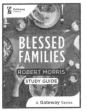

Study Guide: 978-1-949399-55-4
DVD: 978-1-949399-52-3

Study Guide: 978-1-945529-85-6
DVD: 978-1-949399-48-6

Study Guide: 978-1-945529-56-6
DVD: 978-1-949399-43-1

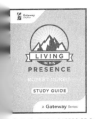

dy Guide: 978-1-945529-55-9
DVD: 978-1-949399-42-4

Study Guide: 978-1-945529-88-7
DVD: 978-1-949399-53-0

Study Guide: 978-1-949399-65-3
DVD: 978-1-949399-66-0

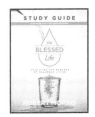

Study Guide: 978-0-997429-84-8
DVD: 978-1-949399-46-2

You can find these resources and others at
www.gatewaypublishing.com

NOTES